MISSION STATEMENT:
A NEW APPROACH TO STATE HISTORY

Each time we prepare to teach Texas history is a perfect time to rethink our approach to teaching it and *The Texas Chronicles* is a tremendous resource to engage the natural curiosity of young learners.

CURIOSITY IS OUR MOST PRECIOUS NATURAL INSTINCT

Throughout history, in most schools, knowledge has been and is still traditionally chopped up into separate subjects (social studies, math, science, etc.) and then further divided into a timetable, syllabus, or curriculum at each grade level.

This is NOT the way the world naturally appears to a child. To a young mind everything is connected, and the real world is often far more fascinating than any story you can make up!

This is particularly the case when it comes to the precious sense of identity and place that young people gain as they progress through their school years prompting them to ask themselves, "Where do I fit in?"

This is why Texas history really matters. Community and state history is the most relevant and easiest for students to connect with. We have a unique opportunity with the publication *The Texas Chronicles* to rethink the way Texas history is taught—not just in social studies or at grades 4 and 7—but all the way through primary and secondary education and across all subject areas.

TIMELINES ARE A FABULOUS FRAMEWORK FOR LEARNING

I have been personally and professionally exploring this educational paradigm for over a decade and here's what I've learned. With a timeline, the arrangement of words and images allow children to explore cross-curricular knowledge through their own natural curiosity—starting wherever they like and making their own journeys through time without ever getting lost or losing context.

Using a timeline also means students can explore a wide spectrum of knowledge through their own interests be it sports, culture, politics, conflict, science, or personalities.

THE TEXAS CHRONICLES IS A PARADIGM SHIFT

It's a new way of looking at Texas history using a timeline and other content created for this very purpose. The timeline unfolds into a six-foot-long wallchart allowing simultaneous multiple users and creating an environment of discussion and debate. It takes readers on a journey through 100 key moments, from the dinosaurs to the present day.

In addition to the timeline, *The Texas Chronicles* features 45 "newspaper" articles, dramatically telling key moments from the state's history as if they happened yesterday. These articles provide a rich bed of content to support select events on the timeline. Finally, on the back of the timeline is a list of key places to visit, a summary of civic government, an honor roll of key figures, and a glossary.

Some historical accounts you and your students will already know, others will be new. Witness the moment of joy when a child discovers they know something their teachers or parents do not! That sense of discovery and joy at becoming an expert is just what I believe develops a love of learning.

THE TEXAS CHRONICLES EDUCATOR'S GUIDE

In the following pages you will find a wide range of activities, ideas, and suggestions on how to use *The Texas Chronicles* in the classroom to enhance the teaching of Texas history for grades K–12. This guide has been created in partnership with experts as well as classroom practitioners and carefully mapped to applicable state standards. Combined with intentional development and professional execution, we hope to infuse Texas educators' lesson plans with high-interest activities and capture the instinctual curiosity of young learners.

Very best wishes,

Christopher Lloyd
World history author and CEO What on Earth Publishing

HOW TO USE THE GUIDE

To aid educators in identifying activities that meet their needs, each activity is coded to the appropriate Texas Essential Knowledge and Skills (TEKS).

SS   Social Studies

LA   English Language Arts and Reading

SC   Science

M   Mathematics

Graphic icons indicate the skills and cross-curricular content. All activities involve social studies content and reading skills to varying degrees, so those items are not represented graphically.

 WRITING

 SPEAKING

 RESEARCH

 MATH

 SCIENCE

Some activities refer to the online resource kit. This is a collection of graphic organizers, sample activities, and links to other resources to help you get the most out of this guide. Find out more information here: whatonearthbooks.com/texas

1 BEHOLD!
THE TIMELINE!

While many of the ideas presented in this resource correspond to specific themes or events in *The Texas Chronicles*, we begin the guide with general suggestions for introducing and using the timeline in the classroom. There are many points of entry into this engaging feature, which we hope will leave students with a greater understanding of the how timelines are constructed and how they allow us to visualize events of the past.

ESSENTIAL QUESTIONS

- What elements are needed to construct an effective timeline?
- What information do timelines help us understand better than text passages?
- How does curated content guide our understanding of the past?

SUGGESTED ACTIVITIES

K–5

 Use mathematical calculations that result in four digit answers to direct students to key dates on the timeline related to important events, in a Scavenger Hunt fashion. An existing example is available in the online resource kit. SS-4.19; M-4.1, 4.4

 Select six articles from *The Texas Chronicles* or events from the timeline and set aside a time, such as every Friday or every other day, to read each one aloud to the class. After each article is read aloud, students should create an illustration of the event (with a descriptive sentence or two, where able). Once all six articles have been read, engage in a class discussion and ask the

The Texas Chronicles timeline

students to arrange their illustrations and descriptions of the six events in order, forming their own mini timelines. Students can share their timeline with a partner or in small groups before sharing with the whole class, thus practicing sequencing. SS-4.19, 4.21; LA-4.1, 4.3, 4.7, 4.11, 4.12

Connect 4: Have students select four moments on the timeline that connect in some way. It is up to the students to determine this connection, and make the case for how they connect. Have them create a graphic organizer, such as a Venn diagram or web of some sort, to show how the moments connect. SS-4.19, 4.21; LA-4.2, 4.3, 4.6, 4.11, 4.12

My Timeline: Create an intergenerational timeline using events from three different generations (grandparent/senior, parent/adult, and events from your own life). Include three important or significant events that happened during each person's lifetime and plot on a timeline. (Be sure to emphasize that if the student does not have access to information about other generations in their families, they can interview neighbors, friends, or consider community resources like nursing homes.) Find and add at least one event on the Texas timeline that connects or adds value to your intergenerational time. Explore your trajectory and your role in history by predicting three significant or important events that will be a part of your future, and can be added to your timeline. SS-4.19, 4.21; LA-4.1, 4.3, 4.7, 4.11, 4.12, 4.13

Time Capsule: After exploring some key Texas history events and figures, gather artifacts, objects, and symbols representing Texas and place them in a time capsule. Imagine this time capsule will be opened in 200 years and you want future Texans to know our history. Be sure to "make the case" for each object as space will be limited. SS-4.19, 4.21; LA-4.2, 4.3, 4.6, 4.11, 4.12

Predict: What will Texas look like in 2219, 200 years from now, in regard to the various categories color-coded on *The Texas Chronicles* timeline (science, culture, sport, etc.)? What event(s) might you plot on a timeline marking notable changes within one of more of these categories? Write and/or draw about your prediction(s) and share with your classmates. Sort the class predictions into the appropriate color-coded categories. Additional connections can be made to the "My Timeline" activity above, by adding their predictions to their intergenerational timeline. SS-4.19, 4.21; LA-4.1, 4.3, 4.7, 4.11, 4.12

An artist's impression
of native peoples
at Guadalupe Bay

Shared Inquiry Extension: After completing their timeline, have the students choose their favorite event(s) to explore. Small groups of students can learn more about a particular event using books or digital resources in a shared research project. The event or subject can be described or summarized in a drawing, written report, or other presentation form. Students may also take on the role of the person they researched, or act out the event they researched, in a living history or living wax museum activity. SS-4.19, 4.21, 4.22; LA-4.1, 4.3, 4.7, 4.11, 4.12, 4.13

After reviewing the timeline, have students, working individually or in groups, select the most important moment from each of the following periods in Texas history: before 1800, 1800–1850, 1850–1900, 1900–1950, and 1950–present. Have students create an illustration of each event (with a descriptive sentence or two, where able) and arrange in chronological order, creating their own mini timeline of important moments in Texas history. Have them share out with the class, justifying why they selected those events. Extension: Have groups notice if the same event or person was selected by multiple groups. Assemble all of the selected important moments, and as a class, engage in discussion and debate to create an overall top 15 moments in Texas history and display the illustrations in timeline form. SS-4.19, 4.21, 4.22; LA-4.1, 4.3, 4.7, 4.11, 4.12

Neil Armstrong taking the first footsteps on the Moon in 1969

7-12

 How Did We Get Here? Have students select, or assign them, an important event on the timeline (tip: select an item on the last half or third of the timeline). Using the articles in *The Texas Chronicles* and the events on the timeline, have them select six items that trace a story culminating in the final important event. SS-7.20, 7.22; LA-7.1, 7.3, 7.5, 7.6

 Identify which events from *The Texas Chronicles* timeline had ripple effects throughout the nation and/or the world. Find corresponding news articles from various perspectives (local, national, global) to make connections and note disparities between the way the event is presented in this account and in the articles found. SS-7.20, 7.22; LA-7.1, 7.3, 7.5, 7.6, 7.12

 What's Left Out?: Explore the timeline, research Texas history, and identify a major event in Texas history that is not included in *The Texas Chronicles*

timeline. Make a case for why it should be included (or excluded), especially in the context of the events which are currently represented. SS-7.20, 7.22; LA-7.1, 7.3, 7.5, 7.6, 7.10, 7.12

After reviewing the timeline, have students, working individually or in groups, select the top five most important moments in Texas history. Have students create an illustration of each event (with a descriptive sentence or two, where able) and arrange in chronological order, creating their own mini timeline of important moments in Texas history. Have them share out with the class, justifying why they selected those events. Extensions: Have groups notice if the same event or person was selected by multiple groups. Assemble all of the selected important moments, and as a class, engage in discussion and debate to create an overall top 15 moments in Texas history and display the illustrations in timeline form. SS-7.20, 7.22; LA-7.1, 7.3, 7.5, 7.6, 7.10

Card Game: Make a copy of the timeline, and cut out and laminate each event to create a set of cards. Depending on the number of students, you may need to make multiple sets of cards and divide the students into small groups to play. Each student group should get one complete "deck" of the timeline cards. Have students deal the cards to their group, keeping their cards hidden. The teacher will call out a term, example "Innovation." The students will examine the cards in their hand, and determine which of the cards they hold fits that term the best, and will play it in the center of their group. Students must then make a case for their card, discuss, justify, and question each other before voting on which of the cards best fits the term. The student who played that card earns a point. Terms that can be used: Progress, Superstar, Change Over Time, Conflict, Persuasive, Hero, Villain, Triumph, Amazing, Exciting, Unbelievable, Groundbreaking, Frightening, etc. SS-7.20, 7.22; LA-7.1, 7.3, 7.5, 7.6

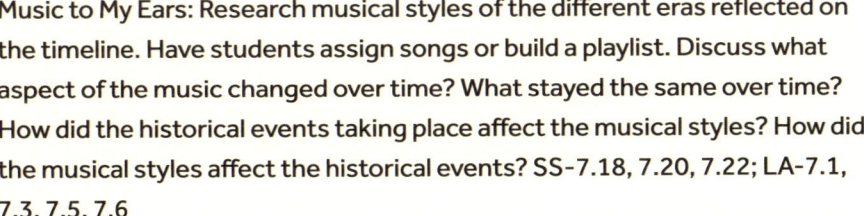

Music to My Ears: Research musical styles of the different eras reflected on the timeline. Have students assign songs or build a playlist. Discuss what aspect of the music changed over time? What stayed the same over time? How did the historical events taking place affect the musical styles? How did the musical styles affect the historical events? SS-7.18, 7.20, 7.22; LA-7.1, 7.3, 7.5, 7.6

2 ENCOUNTERS OF THE TEXAS KIND

Texas history provides many examples of encounters between various groups ranging from contact between Europeans and the first peoples of Texas to those arriving in the 20th century. All of these encounters had aspects in common and yet differed in their own ways. Each was influenced by the physical, social, or political environments in which the encounter took place and the role of those factors should be considered.

ESSENTIAL QUESTIONS

- What were the similarities and differences of various groups involved in encounters?
- How does the environment influence an encounter?
- What are the effects of first contacts between groups?

SUGGESTED ACTIVITIES

K–5

 Using an article from page 7, 11, or 16 of the newspaper, have students create an illustration showing what life was like for the original group before and after the encounter with the new group. SS-4.1, 4.3, 4.4, 4.19, 4.21; LA-4.2, 4.3, 4.6, 4.11, 4.12

 Using articles from pages 1–4, prepare a compare and contrast graphic organizer showing the outlook each group had for the future of Texas. SS-4.1, 4.2, 4.19, 4.21, 5.1; LA-4.2, 4.3, 4.6, 4.11, 4.12

 Using articles from pages 1–4, 7, and 11, prepare a point of view graphic organizer analyzing the chosen article. SS-4.1, 4.2, 4.3, 4.4, 4.19, 4.21; LA-4.2, 4.3, 4.6, 4.11, 4.12

7–12

 Using articles from pages 1–4, 7, and 11, have students prepare for and engage in a panel discussion on the similarities and differences of a selected encounter.

Comanche leader Quanah Parker and his band of warriors

SS-7.1, 7.2, 7.4, 7.6, 7.10, 7.20, 7.22, 8.2;
LA-7.1, 7.3, 7.5, 7.6

 Using the Buffalo Soldier article on page 11, have students discuss various aspects of Frederic Remington's article and illustrations in "The Century" and "Harper's Monthly", including the hardship of cavalry life and the racial environment of the period. Information on the articles and illustrations can be found in the online resource kit. SS-7.6, 7.20, 7.22; LA-7.1, 7.3, 7.5, 7.6

 Using articles on pages 2, 4, 7, or 16, have students compare push and pull factors for two or three different groups who came to Texas. Students should consider economic, social, and political influences on migration. SS-7.2, 7.4, 7.7, 7.10, 7.20, 7.22, 8.2, 8.5, 8.6; LA-7.1, 7.3, 7.5, 7.6

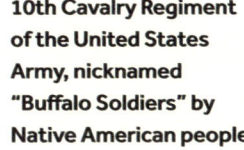
10th Cavalry Regiment of the United States Army, nicknamed "Buffalo Soldiers" by Native American people

  Using all the articles and the timeline, have students compile a list of all the racial and ethnic groups identified. Using other resources, have them research additional groups that came to call Texas home. Then, have individual students or small teams research a recipe for a traditional dish for a chosen group from the list. At a designated time have the students prepare and bring samples of the dish they chose and share with the class how their dish has influenced Texas. SS-7.18, 7.20, 7.22; LA-7.1, 7.3, 7.5, 7.6, 7.12

Using the articles from pages 1–3, have students select an individual or group of people and identify three questions or choices their individual might have as they encountered another group in Texas. Students may record their thinking on a graphic organizer such as the Choices Graphic found in the online resource kit. If students note choices, they could identify which one was actually selected, then describe how history might have been different if another option had been chosen. If they note questions, have students write out the answer to one based on historical evidence. SS-7.1, 7.2, 7.10, 7.20, 7.22, 8.2; LA-7.3, 7.5, 7.6, 7.10

3 FRONTIERS AND FIRSTS

Texas history provides many examples of frontiers and noteworthy firsts. Understanding past frontiers and how people adapted to the challenges associated with them is important to guiding our actions as we continue to approach new frontiers. Whether it be frontiers in settlement, social change, medical technology, or space exploration, each has pioneers, opportunities, and costs that should be understood through the lens of their time.

ESSENTIAL QUESTIONS

- What is a frontier?
- What challenges are associated with a frontier?
- How have frontiers changed Texas?

SUGGESTED ACTIVITIES

K–5

 Using articles from pages 10 or 11, have students construct an infographic describing a selected frontier. SS-4.4, 4.19, 4.21; LA-4.2, 4.3, 4.6, 4.11, 4.12

  Using the Austin article on page 4, discuss the qualifications to receive land in Mexican Texas. Discuss the role of the Certificate of Character in meeting the requirements, then have the students write a Certificate of Character for another student in the class. SS-3.1, 4.2, 4.19, 4.21, 5.4; LA-4.1, 4.2, 4.3, 4.6, 4.7, 4.11, 4.12

 Using the Capitol article on page 12, discuss the challenges of building large structures with simple tools, using the Texas Capitol and San Jacinto Monument as examples. Have students design and build a simple crane to hoist an object to the top of a structure (think Goddess of Liberty statue on top of the Capitol) while exploring the effects of force on an object. SS-4.4, 4.18, 4.19, 4.21; LA-4.1, 4.2, 4.6, 4.7; SC-4.1, 4.2, 4.6

   Using the civil rights article on page 20, discuss with students the concepts of frontiers and firsts then have them identify what about this event/era makes it a frontier or first. Have students brainstorm and research ways this event/era, or other events since, have positively affected or negatively influenced race or cultural relations in Texas. Students can write a press release and hold a press conference to share their findings. Students could also work in pairs to write and conduct an interview, one as the interviewer and one as the interviewee. SS-4.5, 4.19, 4.21, 4.22; 4.1, 4.2, 4.3, 4.6, 4.7, 4.11, 4.12, 4.13

Using the Austin article on page 4, discuss the qualifications to receive land in Mexican Texas. Discuss the amount of acreage available for each man, woman, child, and enslaved person as well as the cost of that land per acre. Have the students calculate the amount of land and the cost for a variety of combinations as well as their own family (see the Land Calculation sheet in the online resource kit.) SS-7.3, 7.20, 7.22; LA-7.1, 7.3, 7.5, 7.6; M-7.1, 7.3

Using the articles on pages 1–4, have the students create an advertisement to get others to move to the frontier. Using all the articles and the timeline, have students select the three most important firsts, and draw a cartoon strip for one or more of their selected firsts. SS-7.1, 7.2, 7.20, 7.22, 8.2; LA-7.3, 7.5, 7.6, 7.10

Texas State Capitol, Austin

Using the article on page 17, have students design a commemorative stamp honoring the achievements of Bessie Coleman. SS-7.7, 7.19, 7.20, 7.22, US.6; LA-7.3, 7.5, 7.6, 7.10

Using the La Salle article on page 2, have students write a persuasive essay. To prepare the essay, make an outline showing their position, three reasons, supporting details (facts and examples) and a concluding statement. Have them address one of the following topics: La Salle should not have traveled to North America; La Salle should have taken a different route to North America; The colonists would have survived if....; or, Even though La Salle failed and most of the colonists died, his expedition influenced the future of Texas. SS-7.1, 7.2, 7.20, 7.22, 8.2; LA-7.3, 7.5, 7.6, 7.10

Using the windmill article on page 13, have students discuss the challenges associated with the Texas climate and the role that access to water has in different regions. Review what else has been done to alter the environment to provide access to water. Have the students develop a plan to ensure that current and future Texans have access to water and then evaluate their plan based on the impact it will have on the environment. SS-7.6, 7.9, 7.10, 7.19, 7.20, 7.22, US.26; LA-7.1, 7.3, 7.5, 7.6, 7.10; SC-7.8, 7.10

Using the Kilby article on page 19, have students further investigate the challenges Jack Kilby was trying to overcome in the invention of the integrated circuit and what its ramifications were. Have students identify at least three challenges humans face that can be resolved by scientific invention. Have students apply scientific investigation and reasoning processes to a possible invention to solve one of their identified challenges. SS-7.7, 7.19, 7.20, 7.22, US.26; LA-7.3, 7.5, 7.12; SC-7.2, 7.3, 7.4

Dallas-based engineer Jack Kilby, inventor of the "integrated circuit"

4 FORTUNE AND FURY

The land and climate of Texas have shaped human activities for thousands of years and continue to do so daily. Natural resources both abundant (energy) and scarce (water) shaped settlement patterns, fueled a vibrant economy, and sparked innovation while the climate demonstrated regularly through hurricanes, tornadoes, and drought just how powerful nature is. Understanding the relationship between Texans and the land is key to being both a good steward and to continuing a tradition of innovation and resilience.

ESSENTIAL QUESTIONS

- How has the environment affected the growth of Texas?
- How have Texans adapted to or modified their environment?
- To what degree has the environment shaped Texas history?

SUGGESTED ACTIVITIES

K–5

 Using the Places to Visit section on the back of the timeline, have students identify five places to visit, and plan a trip to those five places including the combined mileage and the budget for fuel needed for their family car. Have them write why they chose each site and how the environment played a role in that site's existence. SS-4.7, 4.8, 4.9, 4.20, 4.21; LA-4.2, 4.3, 4.6, 4.11, 4.12; M-4.1, 4.2

   Using the article on page 14, have students conduct research on the Great Galveston Storm and identify all the "number" facts in the selection. Students then choose another recent storm or natural disaster in Texas to research and compare similar statistics. Students should focus on geographic and economic factors that influenced or resulted from the event and draw a conclusion about these effects on Texas. SS-4.5, 4.8, 4.11, 4.20, 4.21, 5.8; LA-4.2, 4.3, 4.6, 4.11, 4.12, 4.13; M-4.1, 4.9

Devastation in Galveston after a deadly hurricane in 1900

Using the Spindletop article on page 15, have students research the processes that lead to the existence of crude oil and the forces that cause geysers like Spindletop. Have the students discuss and complete a graphic organizer comparing the positive and negative consequences of fossil fuel exploration and use. SS-4.5, 4.8, 4.11, 4.20, 4.21, 5.5, 5.22; LA-4.1, 4.2, 4.3, 4.6, 4.7, 4.11, 4.12, 4.13; SC-4.7

7-12

Using the article on page 13, have students describe what life would have been like in Texas before and after the innovations described in the article. Which featured innovation had the greatest impact on life in Texas? Why? SS-7.6, 7.8, 7.9, 7.19; LA-7.3, 7.5, 7.6, 7.10

Have students collect evidence on a cause and effect graphic organizer from various articles to respond in paragraph form to the following prompt: Has the Texas environment influenced Texas history overall in a more positive or negative way? Use evidence from the articles to support your conclusion. SS-7.8, 7.9; LA-7.3, 7.5, 7.6, 7.10

Using the cattle article on page 10, have students discuss the reasons for moving cattle to market in Kansas and the risks associated with doing so. Next have the students calculate the revenue and expenses associated with such efforts using word problems, a sample of which is available in the online resource kit. SS-7.5, 7.6, 7.7, 7.12, 7.20, 7.22, US.3; LA-7.1, 7.3, 7.5, 7.6; M-7.1, 7.3

Using the Galveston Hurricane article on page 14, have the students research how Galveston responded to the storm through modification of the environment. Have students identify the costs and benefits of such actions. Have them identify other examples of past, present, and future weather events (i.e. Katrina, Harvey, or climate change) where actions like those in Galveston after the hurricane might be considered. SS-7.7, 7.8, 7.9, 7.20, 7.21, 7.22, US.12; LA-7.1, 7.3, 7.5, 7.6, 7.12; SC-7.8, 7.10

Spindletop near Beaumont, where an oil field was discovered in 1901

Using the Spindletop article on page 15, have the students conduct additional research into the benefits and consequences Texas experienced in the decades following the discovery at Spindletop. Have the students record those benefits and consequences on a graphic organizer. Obtain a container of "Fart Spray" (most brands of this product use sulfur as an active ingredient) online or from a local novelty store to mimic the smell of Texas crude oil which contains significant amounts of sulfur. Disperse a small amount into the air. Once the class's composure has been regained, explain that the smell is a common feature of many Texas oilfield communities. Have the students research the element in Texas crude that gives it that odor and have them explain the processes that caused it to be there. SS-7.7, 7.9, 7.11, 7.12, 7.20, 7.22; LA-7.3, 7.5, 7.6, 7.10, 7.12, US.4, US.15; SC-7.5, 7.6, 7.7, 7.8

5 TEXAS SPIRIT

Texas is recognized across the world in many ways. The way in which the people of Texas are described is sometimes accurate and sometimes misinformed, but it is always changing. To understand what makes Texas unique and the value of that shared distinctiveness, one must understand how that identity has changed over time and how events helped to shape it.

ESSENTIAL QUESTIONS

- What characteristics define a culture?
- What historical turning points have influenced the Texas identity?
- What factors could change the Texas identity of the future?

SUGGESTED ACTIVITIES

K–5

The timeline uses flags to denote different countries and cultures that Texas was associated with over time. Flags are symbols, but today Texas has many officially designated state symbols. Using the Texas State Symbols section of the most recent Texas Almanac, available for free at TexasAlmanac.com, and the articles in *The Texas Chronicles*, have students find five symbols they believe best express the Texas identity. Have them identify the articles with which they believe their chosen symbols best align. Lastly, have them select which official state symbol they believe no longer represents Texas and explain why. Discuss and share their findings. SS-4.14, 4.17, 4.19, 4.21, 5.16; LA-4.1, 4.2, 4.6, 4.7, 4.13

Using the article on page 23, have students create a mini timeline of the big Texas sports highlights and display in a class Exhibition Hall of Fame with items collected and brought from home or illustrated by students. Have students include a plaque that explains why these events define the spirit of Texas. SS-4.17, 4.19, 4.21; LA-4.2, 4.3. 4.6, 4.11, 4.12, 4.13

The Lone Star Flag, adopted as Texas' state flag in 1845

Using the article on page 23, have the students read the article and brainstorm a list of other celebrations unique to Texas (such as Fiesta in San Antonio, Juneteenth, Wurstfest, the Strawberry Festival, etc.). Students can work in groups to research celebrations across the state then plot them on a large wall map of Texas. Students can work together as a class to organize an art gallery of projects created by students illustrating their interpretations of the Texas spirit in these celebrations. SS-3.10, 4.17, 4.19, 4.21, 4.22, 5.21; LA-4.2, 4.3. 4.6, 4.11, 4.12, 4.13

7–12

 Using the articles on pages 1–3, discuss the role Spanish control over Texas had on the Texas culture we know today. Have students identify at least twenty modern reminders of Spanish contributions to Texas culture. From those twenty, have each student identify three items that they feel are most significant and write a persuasive paragraph on why those three are the most important legacies of Spanish contributions to the modern Texas identity. SS-7.2, 7.10, 7.18, 7.20, 7.22; LA-7.3, 7.5, 7.6, 7.10, 7.12

 Following a discussion of the ways in which culture and identity are interconnected, have students select an article that they feel best represents the way Texans today identify themselves. In a paragraph, describe why they chose that article and how it relates to a modern Texas identity. An extension activity might include choosing an article that best represents how others perceive Texans and writing a similar justification. SS-7.18, 7.20, 7.22; LA-7.1, 7.3, 7.5, 7.6, 7.10

  Using the 1936 Centennial item on the timeline as a starting point, have students research the various centennial activities across Texas in 1936. Discuss how the image of the cowboy and the west were highlighted through those celebrations and help shift the identity of Texas from a Southern state to a Western state. In small groups, have the students develop a plan for the Texas Bicentennial in 2036, complete with which activities will take place where and how Texas will be portrayed. Have students present their proposals to a group of teachers, librarians, or administrators to determine the winning proposal. SS-7.7, 7.18, 7.20, 7.22, 7.23; LA-7.1, 7.3, 7.5, 7.6, 7.10, 7.12

A postcard from the Texas Centennial Exposition, held in Dallas in 1936 to commemorate the anniversary of Texas' independence from Mexico

6 ALL OF TEXAS IS A STAGE

Texans have continuously demonstrated their creativity through the arts. From early pictographs to modern examples of visual and performing arts, people across the state of all backgrounds used their talents to reflect the times in which they lived. Their creativity both entertains us and informs our sense of awareness of our surroundings.

ESSENTIAL QUESTIONS

- How do the arts reflect culture?
- How is a period of time reflected through the arts?
- What universal themes are reflected through the arts?

SUGGESTED ACTIVITIES

K–5

 Using the arts article on page 22, the timeline, and the Texas Honor Roll, have the students compile a list of Texas artists from all genres. From that common list, have students draw or select an artist to further research. Students should identify their favorite example of the artist's work, share that example with the class, and write a brief paragraph explaining the basic facts about the artist, any awards they received, and why they chose the specific example of their work. SS-3.12, 4.17, 4.19, 4.21, 5.20; LA-4.2, 4.3, 4.6, 4.11, 4.12, 4.13

Keeping with the theme that "all of Texas is a stage," have students utilize the Place to Visit section and additional research to identify their top ten "theaters" to see a performance. Be sure they don't overlook outdoor venues like Palo Duro Canyon or sporting arenas like Cowboys Stadium or the Alamodome. Their top ten list should identify where it is located, the type of performances hosted there, notable facts like artists who have performed there, and the reason why they placed it on the list in its ranking. SS-4.8, 4.11, 4.17, 4.19, 4.21, 5.20; LA-4.2, 4.3, 4.6, 4.11, 4.12, 4.13

Buddy Holly, who was born in Lubbock and is one of the first rock 'n' roll stars

Using the articles on page 14 and 22, have students compare and contrast (i.e. four commonalities to two differences, or six to three, etc.) the influence of music and culture in two different periods. Students can further research the artists and/or the time period, including other Texan artists or genres of the arts, then create a song, poem, or playlist to demonstrate their findings. SS-4.5, 4.17, 4.19, 4.21, 4.22, 5.20, 5.21; LA-4.2, 4.3, 4.6, 4.11, 4.12, 4.13

7-12

 Have students investigate "how do musicians communicate?" using the article on page 14, about the ragtime music of African American composer Scott Joplin, as an example. They look closely at sheet music for "Scott Joplin's New Rag," and consider what this song would sound like if played. After listening to the historic sound recording of Joplin playing this song, students compare their understandings from observing sheet music and sound recordings. SS-7.18, 7.20, 7.22, US.24, US.25; LA-7.1, 7.3, 7.5, 7.6, 7.12

 Have students in small groups decide on a theme to represent Texas today, then select 3–5 artists to feature on an Austin City Limits show focusing on the theme. Students should explain how work from each selected artist reflects the theme selected and why that theme illustrates Texas today. SS-7.18, 7.20, 7.22; LA-7.1, 7.3, 7.5, 7.6, 7.12

 Have students, in pairs or small groups, research three different episodes of Austin City Limits from three different periods of time. Students should produce a poster, series promotion, or CD cover that describes how the artists from the researched episodes reflected the history of their time. SS-7.18, 7.20, 7.22, 8.26; LA-7.3, 7.5, 7.6, 7.10, 7.12

"King of Ragtime" Scott Joplin, who grew up in Texarkana

7 EXTRAORDINARY TEXANS

Texas history provides many examples of extraordinary individuals who are both well-known and unsung heroes. From those found on the Texas Honor Roll on the back of the timeline to the countless others who have improved their local communities through various acts, all have helped shape Texas. Recognizing the contributions and motivations of others is important in understanding how we as individuals can contribute to making Texas and the world a better place.

ESSENTIAL QUESTIONS

- What qualities or actions make someone extraordinary?
- Would you consider that person's contribution extraordinary today? Why or why not?

SUGGESTED ACTIVITIES

K–5

Students can choose their favorite Texan from one of the many biographical articles, such as Native Americans' Last Stand, Brave Bessie, War Heroes Help America to Victory, 34th President of the U.S., or New Dawn for Civil Rights, and summarize the text. Then they should identify what they think is the most important thing this Texan accomplished and at least two characteristics they believe this person had that made them the "Greatest Texan." Students can then do one of the following activities: create an Extraordinary Character Board for the class showcasing these extraordinary Texans in history by category or chronology; or create a book cover or movie poster advertising the extraordinary Texan, their most important accomplishment, and their most prominent character trait. SS-3.11, 4.2, 4.3, 4.4, 4.5, 4.15, 4.18, 4.19, 4.21, 4.22; LA-4.2, 4.3, 4.6, 4.11, 4.12, 4.13

Have each student select an event or person from the timeline. Using any related articles in *The Texas Chronicles*, books, or digital resources, have them research this person or event. With the information they have gathered, have them prepare for one of the following activities. Human

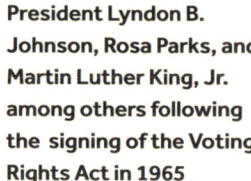

President Lyndon B. Johnson, Rosa Parks, and Martin Luther King, Jr. among others following the signing of the Voting Rights Act in 1965

Timeline: Form a human timeline by having students present their research either in a living history format where students become the character or act out the event, or as though they are in a wax museum where the character only needs to be silent and motionless. Gallery Walk: Have students create visual posters advertising or describing the person or event they researched. SS-4.2, 4.3, 4.4, 4.5, 4.15, 4.18, 4.19, 4.21, 4.22; LA-4.2, 4.3, 4.6, 4.11, 4.12, 4.13

7–12

 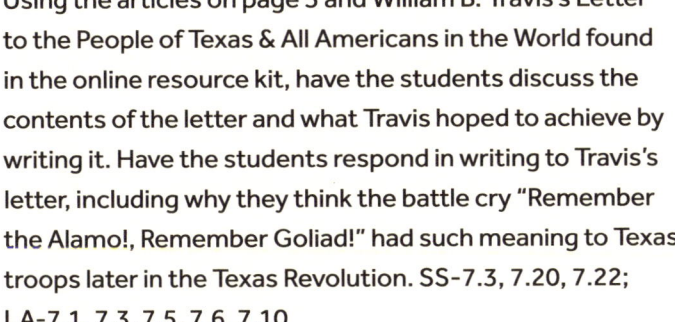 Using the articles on page 5 and William B. Travis's Letter to the People of Texas & All Americans in the World found in the online resource kit, have the students discuss the contents of the letter and what Travis hoped to achieve by writing it. Have the students respond in writing to Travis's letter, including why they think the battle cry "Remember the Alamo!, Remember Goliad!" had such meaning to Texas troops later in the Texas Revolution. SS-7.3, 7.20, 7.22; LA-7.1, 7.3, 7.5, 7.6, 7.10

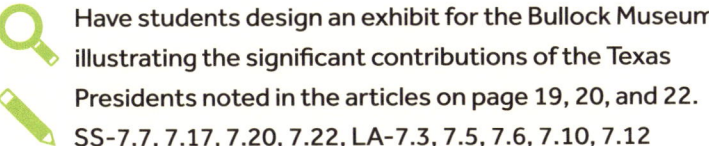 Have students design an exhibit for the Bullock Museum illustrating the significant contributions of the Texas Presidents noted in the articles on page 19, 20, and 22. SS-7.7, 7.17, 7.20, 7.22, LA-7.3, 7.5, 7.6, 7.10, 7.12

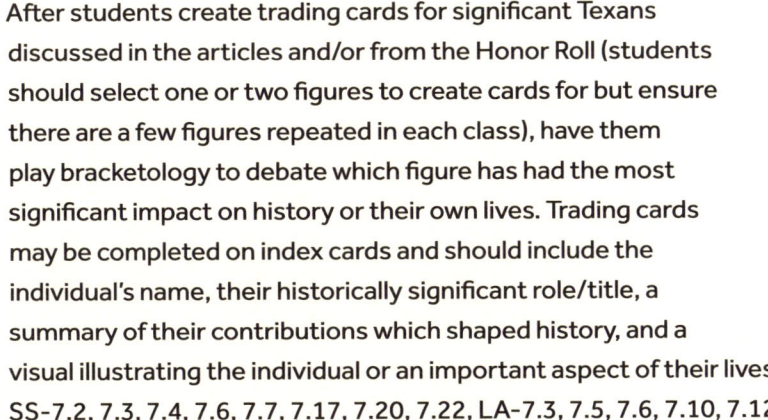 After students create trading cards for significant Texans discussed in the articles and/or from the Honor Roll (students should select one or two figures to create cards for but ensure there are a few figures repeated in each class), have them play bracketology to debate which figure has had the most significant impact on history or their own lives. Trading cards may be completed on index cards and should include the individual's name, their historically significant role/title, a summary of their contributions which shaped history, and a visual illustrating the individual or an important aspect of their lives. SS-7.2, 7.3, 7.4, 7.6, 7.7, 7.17, 7.20, 7.22, LA-7.3, 7.5, 7.6, 7.10, 7.12

 What is in a name? Have students discuss local buildings, streets, and/or memorials that are related to historic Texans featured in the articles and/or Honor Roll. Then have them select and research a local named figure and compare their historic contributions with a similar extraordinary Texan from the book. What qualities or actions make the local noted figure extraordinary? Would you consider that person's contribution extraordinary today? Why or why not? SS-7.2, 7.3, 7.4, 7.6, 7.7, 7.17, 7.20, 7.22, LA-7.1, 7.3, 7.5, 7.6, 7.12

Barbara Jordan, elected to the U.S. House of Representatives in 1972, becoming the first African American woman from a southern state to serve in Congress

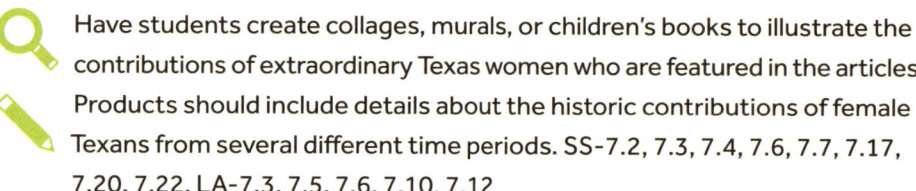 Have students create collages, murals, or children's books to illustrate the contributions of extraordinary Texas women who are featured in the articles. Products should include details about the historic contributions of female Texans from several different time periods. SS-7.2, 7.3, 7.4, 7.6, 7.7, 7.17, 7.20, 7.22, LA-7.3, 7.5, 7.6, 7.10, 7.12

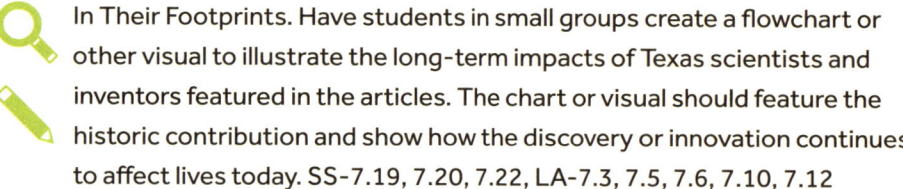 In Their Footprints. Have students in small groups create a flowchart or other visual to illustrate the long-term impacts of Texas scientists and inventors featured in the articles. The chart or visual should feature the historic contribution and show how the discovery or innovation continues to affect lives today. SS-7.19, 7.20, 7.22, LA-7.3, 7.5, 7.6, 7.10, 7.12

In Their Own Words. Challenge students to match a quote to an extraordinary Texan featured in the articles which best reflects the individual's historic contributions. These could be displayed as memes. Students should explain their selection in two or three sentences. SS-7.2, 7.3, 7.4, 7.6, 7.7, 7.17, 7.20, 7.22, LA-7.3, 7.5, 7.6, 7.10, 7.12

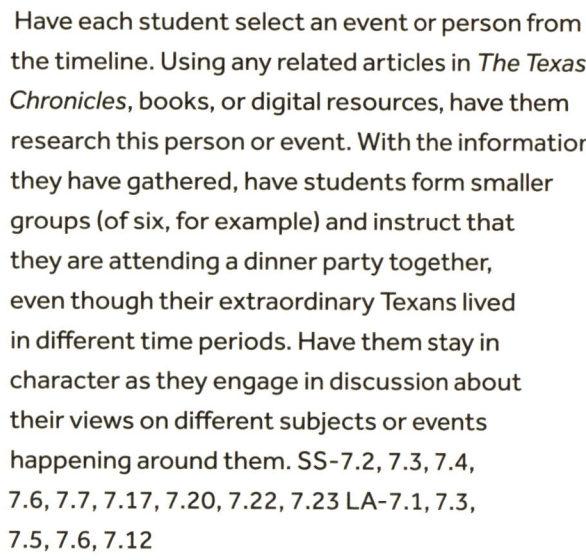 Have each student select an event or person from the timeline. Using any related articles in *The Texas Chronicles*, books, or digital resources, have them research this person or event. With the information they have gathered, have students form smaller groups (of six, for example) and instruct that they are attending a dinner party together, even though their extraordinary Texans lived in different time periods. Have them stay in character as they engage in discussion about their views on different subjects or events happening around them. SS-7.2, 7.3, 7.4, 7.6, 7.7, 7.17, 7.20, 7.22, 7.23 LA-7.1, 7.3, 7.5, 7.6, 7.12

Stephen F. Austin, who founded the first Anglo colony in Texas

8 BEYOND TEXAS

As part of the larger global community, Texas and its people have both been affected by and left their mark on events beyond our borders. This is true from the forces that propelled early exploration and settlement all the way through to the economic and political interdependence we see today. The geographic location, natural resources, and spirit of its people will continue to ensure that Texas will be influential in the United States and beyond.

ESSENTIAL QUESTIONS

- How did world events affect Texas?
- How did Texas contribute to world events?
- What are the most significant influences Texas had on world events?

SUGGESTED ACTIVITIES

K-5

Using the Apollo article on page 21, have students create a three-tab foldable to identify the statements in the article specifically related to Texas (NASA Mission Control, astronauts Ed White and Millie Hughes-Fulford) and the statements related to the world (people around the world watched on TV, a flag and plaque were planted on the Moon) and a third tab for student reflection on how this event has impacted Texas and the world (sacrifices, NASA's Manned Spacecraft Center), even today. This activity could lead to further research about international cooperation, technological innovations, female astronauts, etc. SS-4.5, 4.18, 4.19, 4.21, 5.5; LA- 4.2, 4.3, 4.6, 4.11, 4.12, 4.13; SC-4.3

Using the Bush article on page 22, have students write three facts and a fib about each president, George H. W. Bush and George W. Bush. These can be displayed for the class to view and evaluate through discussion to determine which ones are facts or fibs. Students can then choose one fact related to a policy, vision, or action and research its effect on Texas and/or the world today. SS-4.5, 4.15, 4.16, 4.19, 4.21, 5.5, 5.18; LA- 4.2, 4.3, 4.6, 4.11, 4.12, 4.13

George H. W. Bush and George W. Bush, Texan father and son who both became presidents of the U.S.

Using the WASPs article on page 18, have students choose one of the article topics and create a 4–6 frame comic strip or story board summarizing that section of text. This should be illustrated in color and include accurate facts, in writing or dialogue, in at least half of the frames. SS-3.11, 4.5, 4.19, 4.21, 5.5; LA- 4.2, 4.3, 4.6, 4.11, 4.12

7–12

 Using the article on page 9, have students compare Juneteenth celebrations to Fourth of July celebrations, using a Venn diagram. What events take place on the two days? What do people do? How are the events described in the media? When students notice differences between the celebrations, ask them to hypothesize about the reasons. Conclude the discussion by asking students what conclusions they can draw about the ways that people celebrate and define freedom in America. SS-7.5, 7.18, 7.20, 7.22; LA-7.1, 7.3, 7.5, 7.6, 7.10

 Using German Plot Threatens Texas article on page 15, have students place the events described into a graphic organizer, like the Beginning, Middle, or End graphic found in the online resource kit. Then instruct them to use their understanding of events around WWI to write out the remaining two parts of the story. SS-7.7, 7.20, 7.22 US.4; LA-7.3, 7.5, 7.6, 7.10

 Have students select any one of the individuals named in any of the articles on page 18, and create either an inner monologue, sensory figure, or trading card graphic which highlights their experiences during WWII. An inner monologue and sensory figure graphic example can be found in the online resource kit. In groups, have students compare experiences and summarize significant contributions of key individuals. SS-7.7, 7.20, 7.22, 7.23, US.7; LA-7.1, 7.3, 7.5, 7.6, 7.10

 Have students create a "History through the Texas Lens" timeline, infographic, or story of their choice. The product should summarize the key details of one or more historic events featured in articles from the Texas, U.S., and World views. SS-7.2, 7.3, 7.4, 7.5, 7.6, 7.7, 7.20, 7.22; LA-7.3, 7.5, 7.6, 7.10

Women's Airforce Service Pilots (WASPs), who were trained as pilots to support the U.S. military campaign in World War II